Reverend **JOHN WESLEY**, M.A.

THE RIGHT WAY TO USE MONEY

Reprinted from

SERMONS ON SEVERAL OCCASIONS
Translated into Modern English

By
James D. Holway M.A.,B.D.,Ph.D.

MOORLEYS
Print & Publishing
tel: 0115 932 0643   web: www.moorleys.co.uk

British Library Cataloguing in Publication Data.
A catalogue record for this book is available
from the British Library.

ISBN 978 086071 529 0

MOORLEYS
Print & Publishing
tel: 0115 932 0643 web: www.moorleys.co.uk

PUBLISHER'S NOTE

Our ever popular "SERMONS ON SEVERAL OCCASIONS", translated into Modern English by James D. Holway, has brought a fresh interest in Wesley's Sermons to many. From its modest beginnings of a publication using the original printouts from the Translator's Amstrad word-processor it is now available re-set in a clear typeface and the binding is sewn for added durability.

Not long after its original publication Margaret Thatcher, then Prime Minister, quoted from Wesley's sermon 44 in a debate in Parliament. The then Secretary of the Division for Social Responsibility of the Methodist Church encouraged us to publish this sermon separately so that the full extent of Wesley's advice could be easily accessible.

This present booklet is extracted from the 2nd edition of "Sermons" which is available through all good Bookshops or direct from our Mail Order Department.

THE RIGHT WAY TO USE MONEY   (576)

(The use of money)

Jesus said, 'And so I tell you: make friends for yourselves with worldly wealth, so that when it gives out, you will be welcomed in the eternal home.'
Luke 16.9.

The story of the shrewd manager

1.   Jesus was accused of making friends with sinners and immoral people, and so he told his accusers the parable of the prodigal son (Lk 15.11-32). He then went on to tell another story, this time to his own followers:

> He said to his disciples, 'There was once a rich man who had a servant who managed his property. The rich man was told that the manager was wasting his master's money, so he called him in and said, "What is this I hear about you? Hand in a complete account of your handling of my property, because you cannot be my manager any longer." (Lk 16.1-2).

Jesus proceeded to describe the way in which the bad manager tried to provide for his uncertain future, and how the man's master praised him for his shrewd course of action. Then Jesus makes this telling comment:

> the people of this world are much more shrewd in handling their affairs than the people who belong to the light. (Lk 16.8).

In other words, those who don't look beyond the visible world are wiser than those who see God's glory shining in the face of Jesus. (2 Cor 4.6). Now, they are hardly wiser in any *absolute* sense, for in their rejection of God I consider them utterly stupid idiots, but they are wiser in the sense that they are more consistent with themselves, they are truer to their own principles, and they are more single-minded in pursuing their aims.

Mammon (577)

Jesus then gives us the words of our text. In effect he says,

I am the Son of God, the creator, Lord and possessor of heaven and earth, the judge of all. One of these days when you have finished managing my property, I shall expect an account from you of how you have handled it. But for the present, I tell you, learn something from the dishonest manager. Make friends for yourselves by means of worldly wealth.

Mammon in the original Aramaic means *wealth*. In the older versions it was described as 'the mammon of unrighteousness' because of the wrong way in which money may be obtained and used. 'Make yourself friends with this', says Jesus, 'by doing all possible good, particularly to the children of God, so that when you die, some of those who have gone before you may welcome you into the eternal home.'

The right use of money

2.   In this passage Jesus is teaching all his followers a very important lesson, namely, how to use money in the right way. Usually it is men of the world who speak on this subject, and they do so from their own point of view. Christians don't often give it much thought. I believe that the Lord's people should pay more attention to money and how to use it to the best advantage. The invention of money is just one example of God's wisdom and gracious providence to us. Poets and orators in every time and place have railed at money as the root of all evil. The Roman poet Ovid described gold as

more mischievous than keenest steel.
(Ovid, *Metamorphoses*, I.i.141).

He complained that

wealth is dug up, an incentive to all ill.
(*Ibid*. I.i.140).

Another Roman poet, this time Horace, advised his country men to throw all their money into the sea in order to banish all vice. (Horace, *Odes*, III.xxiv.47-49). But there is no reason for this assumption that money is evil.

The world is corrupt, but silver and gold are not to blame. It is the *love* of money, not money itself, which is the root of all evil, according to Paul. (1 Tim 6.10). The fault does not lie in the money but in the people who use it. Money can be misused, but so can everything else in this world. It can also be used in the right way.

Money a medium of exchange (578)

Money is indispensable to the everyday life of civilised nations. It is versatile, and if Christians use it wisely it can serve many good purposes. It is true that if we live like Adam and Eve, or if we were all filled with the Holy Spirit and lived like the people in the early church in Jerusalem, then we should have all things in common and we should not need to use money. I cannot imagine it being used in heaven. But in mankind's present state, money is a gift from God for us to use as a medium of exchange. It provides the needy with food and drink, clothing and shelter. Christians can use money to help widows and orphans, the sick and the oppressed, the blind and the lame. Money can bring people back from death's door to health and strength again.

Three simple rules

3.   It is important, therefore, that all Christians should know how to use money in the right way. I am going to reduce the many words of advice on this subject to three simple rules. If we keep them we can claim to be faithful managers of our money:

I.	Earn all you can,
II.	Save all you can,
III.	Give all you can.

I. EARN ALL YOU CAN (579)

Earn all the money you can

I.1.   The first of these rules is this: Earn all the money you can. This is the sort of language that worldly people understand. It is our duty to earn all the money we can, with certain conditions, of course. Even money has its price, and sometimes it can be bought too dearly. For example, we ought not to earn our income at the cost of life or limb. We ought not to take a job which results in our ruining our health or which deprives us of adequate time for eating and sleeping. Occupations differ considerably in this respect. Some are totally unhealthy, such as working with arsenic and lead or other dangerous chemicals. Others can be done by stronger people but not by the weak. Sedentary jobs, for example, require long hours sitting down writing in an awkward posture. Whatever it is which is bad for our health, we ought to remember that life is 'worth more than food' and the body is 'worth more than clothes.' (Mt 6.25). If we are already working in an unhealthy job we should change it for another, even if it is not paid so well.

But not at the expense of conscience

2.   Secondly, we must earn as much as we can, but not if it troubles our conscience. We must preserve both physical and spiritual health. Therefore we must not take a job which involves breaking the laws of God or the laws of the State. I am thinking here particularly of work which involves tax evasion. It is just as wrong to defraud the State as it is to defraud your neighbour. The government has as much right to public property as we have to our personal property.

Then again there are other questionable businesses. Although they may be acceptable in themselves they may not bring in an adequate return without cheating or lying or following doubtful business practices. Keep away from this sort of occupation. We must not earn a living at the expense of our souls.

A matter for the individual conscience   (580)

There are certain occupations which are quite harmless for some people but not for others. A job might bring you into contact with undesirable company, and however hard you try you cannot separate the job from the personnel. Or there may be something about the work which makes it a particular temptation for you. To give a personal illustration, I have often wanted to study mathematics, but I am convinced that if I did become a mathematician it would turn me into a Deist or an atheist. Yet I know of Christian mathematicians. So one person cannot lay down rules for another; we must all judge for ourselves and keep away from things which hurt the soul.

Not at the expense of our neighbour's wealth

3.   Thirdly, we must not earn our living by hurting our neighbours. We must not grow rich at the expense of another's wealth. We must not eat up other people's profits, or their capital, by gambling, or by allowing debts to run up, or by charging high rates of interest on loans to them.   All pawnbroking is excluded. The evil it causes far outweighs any good it might do.   Undercutting a rival's prices is also excluded since we must not ruin a neighbour's trade in order to advance our own. We may not take on extra workers if they are still needed by their present employer. Earning money at the expense of someone else's wealth is the same as earning damnation.

Not at the expense of our neighbour's health   (581)

4.   Nor must we earn our living by injuring our neighbour's health. This means particularly that Christians should have nothing to do with the sale of strong drink.   It is true that spirits are sometimes prescribed as medicines, generally by unskilled doctors, so that the small number of people who prepare and sell spirits for medical purposes may do so with a clear conscience.   But the multitude of sellers of strong drink are all public poisoners. They murder their fellow citizens and send them to hell in droves. Who would envy them their large estates and fine palaces bought with the blood of their customers?   God's curse is on their timber, stones and furniture.   God's curse is on their gardens, parks and avenues.   Their foundations, walls and roofs are all stained with blood. They think that they will pass on all this wealth to their descendants. Not so, for God in heaven will soon root them out. They have destroyed the people with their strong drink, and God in turn will make their wealth perish with them.

Not at the expense of our neighbour's body

5.   Workers in the health services experience the same temptation to play with people's lives in order to enlarge their own incomes. They may delay treating patients in order to earn more money. They may lengthen the time taken to cure a complaint when they could treat it quickly. Health workers must have it on their consciences if they do not remove all sickness and pain as soon as they can. Otherwise where is their love for their neighbour? We should each remember to do to others what we would hope they would do to us.

Not at the expense of our neighbour's soul (582)

6.   We must not earn our wages at the risk of injuring our neighbour's soul by providing an opportunity for immorality or intemperance. No Christian can have any part in these activities. If your job has anything to do with public houses or theatres, or any other leisure activity, you should ask yourself whether your work helps or hinders human souls. If it helps them then your employment is good and your conscience is clear. But if your work is sinful in itself, or if it encourages sin in others, then beware. One day God will say to you 'They were still sinners when they died, and I hold you responsible for their deaths.' (cf. Ezek 33.8).

Do not waste your time

7.   I have now run through various cautions and restrictions on Christian employment. Bearing these in mind let me return to the first and greatest rule of Christian wisdom about money, namely, 'Earn all you can.' Earn all you can by honest industry. Work hard at your job. Don't waste time. If you understand yourself and your relationship with God and your neighbour you will know that you do not have any time to waste. And if you understand your work properly you will never have time hanging on your hands. All work expands to fill the time available for it. If you are determined to earn your money honestly you will not be tempted to waste your time. You will always be able to find something worth doing. 'Work hard at whatever you do.' (Ecc 9.10). Do it as soon as possible. Don't put things off from one day to the next. Never leave to tomorrow what can be done today. And do it to the best of your ability. Don't sleep or yawn over your work. Put your mind to it. Don't do things by halves. Don't skimp your work, finish the job.

Efficiency in your work (583)

8.   Keep your mind alert when you are working. Use the intelligence and common sense which God has given you. It is amazing to observe how few people do this and how many of them just carry on doing what others have done before them. Custom and tradition are not hard and fast rules for Christians. You should try and improve whatever you are doing. You ought to be learning continually from your experience and the experience of others. Put into practice what you learn so that what you do today is always an improvement on what you did yesterday.

II. SAVE ALL YOU CAN

Don't waste your money

II.1.   Having earned all you can by honest toil, the second rule of Christian prudence is this: save all you can. Don't throw your money into the sea. Don't throw it away on impulse spending. Don't waste it on worthless luxuries or on an extravagant life style.

2.   Don't waste your precious money on bodily luxuries. Any sensible heathen would condemn gluttony and drunkenness. I would take it further and condemn elegant living and conspicuous consumption. Don't cultivate an expensive life style. Cut out unnecessary expense and be content with a simple way of life.

3.   Don't waste your money on unnecessary clothes and ornaments. Don't fill your house with expensive furniture, or paintings or books. Make your garden useful rather than elegant. Don't try to keep up with your neighbours. They can spend their money wastefully if they choose. 'Follow me,' says Jesus, 'and let the dead bury their own dead.' (Mt 8.22). If you really intend to follow Jesus in this respect you will find yourself able to do so.

Status symbols   (584)

4.   Don't waste your money on buying status symbols, things which you hope will arouse the admiration or envy of your neighbours. Spending money in this way is often the result of pride. People try to live at a high standard in order to gratify their vanity. 'A man ... is praised because he is successful.' (Ps 49.18). Wealthy people will let you rub shoulders with them as long as you share their attitudes and life style. Don't set great store by their applause. It is better to seek God's approval.

Insatiable wants

5.   One problem which accompanies the attempt to live in luxury is that human wants are never satisfied. Daily experience shows that our expectations are always rising. Whenever you spend your money on a personal indulgence you are paying some of it to sensuality as a kind of tax. If you buy something which is attractive to look at, a proportion of the money goes on the attractiveness. If you buy something to win the approval of your

friends you are spending some of the money on buying vanity. This is a foolish way to carry on. In effect you are using your money to buy more of your vices. It would be better to throw it into the sea.

Bequests   (585)

When you spend your money on your children the result is the same. You buy them more temptation and vices.

7.   Don't leave your money to your children unless they know how to use it wisely. If you think that it will become a snare to them, take pity on them and spare them the temptation. I am amazed at the infatuation of some parents. They think that they can never leave their children enough money. Having become slaves of pride, vanity and ambition themselves, they do their best to enslave their children as well. So, both parents and children will end in hell, well supplied with 'the worms that eat them ... and the fire that burns them.' (Mk 9.48).

8.   Parents ask me, 'What would you do if you were in my position and you had a considerable fortune to leave?'
        Well, circumstances alter cases, and I don't know what I *would* do, but I know very well what I *ought* to do. If only one of my children knew the value of money and would put it to good use, I would give the bulk of my fortune to that one child and leave the others just enough to keep them at their present standard of living. If none of my children knew how to use money properly, hard as it sounds, I would make adequate provision for each one and then bequeath the remainder to other purposes which I thought would best glorify God.

III. GIVE ALL YOU CAN

Do not let money lie idle

III.1.   Earning all you can and saving all you can may seem adequate advice, but we cannot stop there. You can hardly be said to save money if you only keep it in a safe. You might as well throw it into the sea or bury it in the earth or lock it in a chest or put it in the Bank of England. Not to use money is in effect the same as throwing it away. If you would really 'make friends for yourselves with worldly wealth' then you must add a third rule. Having first earned all you can and secondly saved all you can, then thirdly you must give away as much as you can.

Goods held in trust (586)

2. Why must you give all you can? I want to remind you that the whole universe belongs to God. When he created you and brought you into this world he intended you to be a steward or manager, not an owner. He placed various goods in your trust for a while, but they still belong to him. You yourself belong to him, body and soul, and so do all the things you call your own. God has told you very clearly that you are to use your wealth in such a way that it may be an acceptable offering to him through Jesus. This is a task he wants us to perform for him, and the reward he has promised for doing this work is eternal glory.

Instructions for use

3. Here are the instructions which God has given you about how you should use your worldly goods. God has lent them to you, and if you wish to use them in the way he intended the first thing to do is to provide for your needs: food to eat and clothes to wear, enough to keep you healthy. Secondly, provide for the needs of your wife and children and servants and anyone else in your household. If there is any money left over, then do good 'to those who belong to our family in the faith.' (Gal 6.10). If there is any left after this, 'as often as we have the chance, we should do good to everyone.' (Gal 6.10). In doing this you give all you can, indeed you give all you have, for all that you have allocated in this way is really given to God. You 'pay God what belongs to God,' (Mt 22.21), not only by what you give to the poor, but also by what you spend in providing for the needs of yourself and your household.

A four-fold consideration (587)

4. So if you are in doubt at any time about what you are going to spend on any part of your family, calmly ask yourself,

Firstly, in spending this money am I behaving as though I owned it, or as though I were managing it for God?

Secondly, am I doing this in obedience to his word? Where in the Bible does it tell me to do this?

Thirdly, can I present this action to God as a task done for him through Jesus?

Fourthly, do I believe that what I am doing will merit a reward in heaven?

These four questions should give you clear guidance about what you ought to do.

Resort to prayer

5.   But if you are still in doubt, then you should examine your motives prayerfully. Can you say in the Spirit,

> Lord, you know that I am thinking of buying this food, or clothing, or furniture. You know that I am trying to be a good manager of the money you have given me. You know that I have been guided by your Word in taking this course of action. Grant that what I am doing will be acceptable to you through Jesus. And may your Holy Spirit assure me that this labour of love will be rewarded in the hereafter.

If, after offering this prayer, you receive the assurance of the Holy Spirit, then you may go ahead in the knowledge that you are doing God's will.

Summary   (588)

6.   You should now be able to see what it means to 'make friends for yourselves with worldly wealth,' and what you have to do 'so that when it gives out, you will be welcomed in the eternal home.' I have explained to you the nature and extent of Christian prudence in financial matters. Earn all you can with diligence and application, without hurting either yourself or your neighbour in body or soul. Save all you can by not spending money on foolish temptations. Don't waste your money on unnecessary consumption, whether for yourself or your family. Then, having done this, give all you can, that is, give all you have to God. Do not stint yourself. Do not give God a tenth, or a third, or a half. Give him everything you have, whether it is much or little, by spending it on yourself, your family, your fellow-Christians, and the rest of mankind, in that order, in such a way that when your life is over you may look back and see your trust from God faithfully discharged. Your stewardship should have been in accordance with the Bible, acceptable as a sacrificial offering to God, and deserving a reward when the Lord returns.

Conclusion

7.　　　There is no other way for us to be good managers of our Lord's goods. The Bible and our own conscience make that clear. So why delay? Why continue to treat your money in a selfish worldly way? Our kingdom and our wisdom are not of this world. Worldly customs should carry no weight with us. We should follow other people's advice only so far as they give Christian advice. Listen instead to the words of Jesus. At this very moment I urge you in the name of Jesus to use your money in a Christian way. No more laziness! No more slacking on the job, no more waste of time, no more wasteful spending of money, no more covetousness. Use whatever money God has entrusted you with in helping your fellow-Christians and all in need. Give all that you have, as well as all that you are, as an offering to God. Remember he gave us his only Son. Christians who fully commit themselves in this way will 'store up for themselves a treasure which will be a solid foundation for the future. And then they will be able to win the life which is true life.' (1 Tim 6.19).

MOORLEYS
Print & Publishing

As a well established publisher we add several new titles to our list each year.
We also undertake private publications and commissioned works.

Our range includes

Books of Verse
Devotional Poetry
Recitations for Children
Humorous Monologues

Drama
Bible Plays
Sketches
Christmas, Passiontide,
Easter & Harvest Plays
Demonstrations

Resource Books
Assembly Material
Easy Use Music Books for Piano and Keyboard
Children's Addresses
Prayers
Worship & Preaching
Books for Speakers

Activity Books
Quizzes & Puzzles

Church Stationery
Notice Books & Cradle Roll Certificates

Associated Lists and Imprints
Cliff College Publishing
Nimbus Press
MET (Headway)
Social Work Christian Fellowship

**For up to date news, special offers & information on our full
list of titles, please visit our website at www.moorleys.co.uk**

Alternatively send a stamped addressed C5 envelope for our current catalogue, or consult
your local Christian Bookshop, who will either stock or be able to obtain our titles.